הבנין ליה דמיתבעא
אחוי ליד ובתאי
לחיי
מלאך המות
הבלי
סכינא

The Legend of Rabbi Ben Levi

From "Tales of a Wayside Inn"

By Henry Wadsworth Longfellow

Illustrated by Avi Katz

We would like to thank The Israel Antiquities Authority and its Head Yisrael Hasson, the Jezreel Valley Local Council, Archeologist Professor Mordecai Aviam, and Restorer Yeshu Dray for their help and cooperation in restoring the site of the Tomb of Rabbi Yehoshua Bar Lavi in Zippori. Anat Avital for her photographs of the Zippori mosaics. Ilan Hills for photography of the Ribal mosaic Ilana Kurshan for aid in some of the Aramaic translations.

Copyright © Avi Katz
Jerusalem 2020/5781

All rights reserved. No part of this publication may be translated, reproduced, stored in a retrieval system or transmitted, in any form or by any means, electronic, mechanical, photocopying, recording or otherwise, without express written permission from the publishers.

Cover Design: Leah Ben Avraham/Noonim Graphics
Typesetting: Estie Dishon

ISBN: 978-965-7023-54-9

1 3 5 7 9 8 6 4 2

Gefen Publishing House Ltd.
6 Hatzvi Street
Jerusalem 9438614
Israel
972-2-538-0247
orders@gefenpublishing.com

Gefen Books
c/o Baker & Taylor Publisher Services
30 Amberwood Parkway
Ashland, Ohio 44805
516-593-1234
orders@gefenpublishing.com

www.gefenpublishing.com

Printed in Israel

Library of Congress Control Number: 2020915510

The Legend of Rabbi Ben Levi

From "Tales of a Wayside Inn"

By Henry Wadsworth Longfellow
Illustrated by Avi Katz

gefen
publishing house
JERUSALEM • NEW YORK
Est. 1981

WHAT IS A MIRACLE?

A miracle breaches the laws of nature; it is a direct intervention into reality by God. The Jewish sages were split on the issue: Were miracles "programmed" into reality (per Maimonides), or were they violations of reality? Either way, as Rabbi Ben Levi in this poem shows, the Jewish sages felt quite comfortable appealing directly to God when they desired a miracle. Jewish legend is filled with such tales – as, of course, is the New Testament. Like the sages, Jesus of Nazareth (a small village outside Zippori) performs miracles: he calms the storm over the Sea of Galilee by rebuking it, and he casts the demons of the Gerasene into a herd of swine. This may be one explanation for the fascination Longfellow held for the strange Jewish tale of Rabbi Ben Levi and his journey to the afterworld.

Miracles are breaches in reality. Both the prophet Elijah and his disciple, Elisha, casually raise the dead (purely as a courtesy to their respective hosts!), while the so-called Witch of Endor, in her turn, summons the spirit of the prophet Samuel at the behest of King Saul. Death might be a mystery, but to the sages it was a practical one. Longfellow, who lost two wives to the Angel of Death, no doubt had that in mind when he sat down to write this poem, in which Rabbi Ben Levi is offered, uniquely, a glimpse of the afterlife. It wrestles with the question of death, to which there is no answer, and acknowledges at last the futility of the thing that, as another great poet put it, we know we can't escape yet can't accept (Philip Larkin, "Aubade").

In this slim volume, the artist Avi Katz has reimagined the Longfellow poem and the legend of Ben Levi in a series of mosaic paintings that bring the tale to

8

vivid life, featuring excerpts from the Talmudic text (*Ketubot* 77b) in which the story of Rabbi Ben Levi (or Bar Levi, as it says in the original Aramaic) is found. The rabbi himself has long since departed this mortal realm and no doubt resides beside God in that Celestial Town he visited once in life. His grave is on this earth, yet his spirit is elsewhere – but you may take comfort in the splendid views of his resting place and in the gorgeous art his tale inspires.

Lavie Tidhar
2020

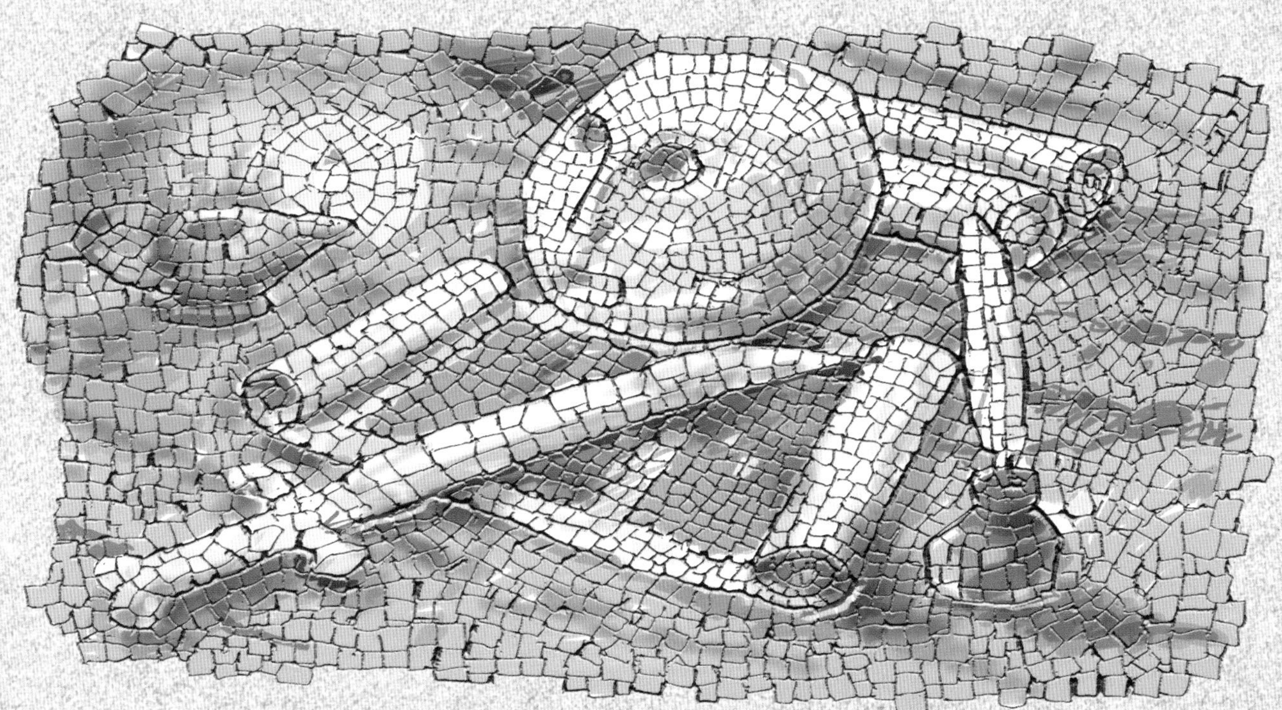

Rabbi Ben Levi, on the Sabbath, read
A volume of the Law, in which it said,
"No man shall look upon my face and live."
And as he read, he prayed that God would give
His faithful servant grace with mortal eye
To look upon His face and yet not die.

רבי יהושע בר לוי
Rabbi Yehoshua Bar Levi

Then fell a sudden shadow on the page,
And lifting up his eyes, grown dim with age,
He saw the Angel of Death before him stand,
Holding a naked sword in his right hand.

אזל איתחזי ליה
Appeared before him

אני אברהם אביך

Rabbi Ben Levi was a righteous man,
Yet through his veins a chill of terror ran,
With trembling voice he said, "What wilt thou here?"
The Angel answered, "Lo! the time draws near
When thou must die; yet first, by God's decree,
Whate'er thou askest shall be granted thee."
Replied the Rabbi, "Let these living eyes
First look upon my place in Paradise."

מלאך המות
The Angel of Death

מלאך
המוות

Then said the Angel, "Come with me and look."
Rabbi Ben Levi closed the sacred book,
And rising, and uplifting his gray head,
"Give me thy sword," he to the Angel said,
"Lest thou shouldst fall upon me by the way."
The Angel smiled and hastened to obey,

אחוי לי דוכתא - הב לי סכינך
Show me my place - give me your knife.

אל תדין את חברך
עד שתגיע למקומו

Then led him forth to the Celestial Town,
And set him on the wall, whence gazing down,
Rabbi Ben Levi, with his living eyes,
Might look upon his place in Paradise.

קא מַחֲזִי לֵיהּ
He showed it to him

דוד והאריה

Then straight into the city of the Lord
The Rabbi leaped with the Death Angel's sword,
And through the streets there swept a sudden breath
Of something there unknown, which men call death.

בשבועתא דלא אתינא
I swear that I will return

Meanwhile the Angel stayed without, and cried,
"Come back!" To which the Rabbi's voice replied,
"No! in the name of God, whom I adore,
I swear that hence I will depart no more!"

הב לי סכינאי
Give me my knife!

Then all the Angels cried, "O Holy One,
See what the son of Levi here has done!
The kingdom of Heaven he takes by violence,
And in Thy name refuses to go hence!"
The Lord replied, "My Angels, be not wroth;
Did e'er the son of Levi break his oath?
Let him remain; for he with mortal eye
Shall look upon my face and yet not die."

ניהדר אי לא
He must return...if not...

הילדים אל לא

Beyond the outer wall the Angel of Death
Heard the great voice, and said, with panting breath,
"Give back the sword, and let me go my way."
Whereat the Rabbi paused and answered, "Nay!
Anguish enough already has it caused
Among the sons of men!" And while he paused,
He heard the awful mandate of the Lord
Resounding through the air, "Give back the sword!"

נפקא בת קול
A voice was heard

בריחת
יונה

The Rabbi bowed his head in silent prayer;
Then said he to the dreadful Angel, "Swear,
No human eye shall look on it again;
But when thou takest away the souls of men,
Thyself unseen and with an unseen sword
Thou wilt perform the bidding of the Lord."

סכינאי - סכינך

My knife - your knife

סכינאי סכינך

The Angel took the sword again, and swore,
And walks on earth unseen forevermore.

ניהליה דמיתבעא לברייתא

It is necessary for the death of mortals

לכהן הגדל דזמינת אלעזר
פרן גמלא

Rabbi Yehoshua Ben Levi

Sometime in the middle of the third century CE, Rabbi Yehoshua Ben Levi lived in Zippori, the ancient Jewish capital of the Galilee, and then he was gone.

There were two clues to his disappearance, one a legend and the other a tomb. The legend of Rabbi Yehoshua Ben Levi, also known as the Ribal, and his encounter with the Angel of Death appears not only in the Talmud (*Ketubot* 77b), but in dozens of other versions in many cultures, including even the Islamic Koran. He is revered in Jewish Scripture as being one of the few righteous souls allowed to enter Paradise while still alive.

On a hillside facing the remains of ancient Zippori, in the early twenty-first century, a cave tomb was discovered bearing the inscription "Here is the resting place of Rabbi Yehoshua Ben Levi." Inside the perfectly preserved burial chamber are the niches for six tombs. Five contain the untouched remains of the original occupants, over eighteen hundred years old. Yet one crypt remains mysteriously empty, its inhabitant long gone or never there.

The earthly Rabbi Yehoshua Ben Levi was a well-known historical figure in the third-century Galilee. The Jewish community flourished under the leadership of Rabbi Yehuda Hanasi. He gathered all the great scholars of the day, including the Ribal, in Zippori to create a compilation of Jewish law in the book that became known as the Mishnah. This became the basis of the laws that guide Jewish communities throughout the world to this day. He is mentioned dozens of times in Talmudic literature as an authority in halachah (Jewish law) and was a leading political figure as well, traveling as far as Rome to represent the Jewish people against the imperial forces of Roman occupation.

The sources present the Ribal as a modest man who found his place among the common people. When the plague of leprosy was at its height, other rabbis recommended quarantine, distance, or even exiling the unfortunate victims. But the Ribal instead sought them out and would sit with them, teaching Scripture, believing that this kindness would provide the greatest protection against any disease.

The mystical Rabbi Yehoshua Ben Levi was the equivalent of an ancient comic book hero. Jewish legend abounds in tales of how he joined with his mentor Elijah the Prophet, the duo serving as a sort of Talmudic Batman and Robin, traveling the world dispensing justice and mercy. There is also a famous tale of Elijah sending the Ribal to the gates of Rome to meet the Messiah and attempt to hasten his arrival.

Zippori holds a unique status among the ancient cities of Israel. While the official founding of the town by Jews returning from the Persian exile is dated to the fifth century BCE, Talmudic sources claim that the town, then known as Kitron, dates from the time of Joshua and was surrounded by a wall. Archeologists have also discovered the foundations of dozens of stone homes dating from the Neolithic period, over ten thousand years ago, making Zippori one of the oldest inhabited sites in Israel. It has also been continually inhabited throughout its history, with one civilization blending into the next as history marched forward. Only the name was modified over time, from Zippori to Sepphoris to Le Safourie to Safuriyya and back to Moshav Zippori today.

My family came – myself originally from New York City and my wife from Denver – to Zippori in 1991 and found land on an abandoned hillside containing a ruined house and weeds as thick as a jungle. But the view was beautiful, and the potential was there. We went to work. We planted pomegranate and olive trees and made honey and wine. We built guest houses for people to come and visit the brand new Zippori National Park, which had opened on the hillside facing us.

The ground was full of cut stones, evidence of thousands of years of home builders, and we mined the land for these stones to build our own house. One day, while clearing stones from a terrace, we uncovered the opening to a cave. The entrance was protected by an inscribed stone door proclaiming, "Here is the tomb of Rabbi Yehoshua Ben Levi."

According to Israeli law, all ancient discoveries fall under the jurisdiction of the Israel Antiquities Authority (IAA). Following our initial excitement, we contacted them. This was the beginning of a saga that lasted many years and ended in the courthouses in nearby Nazareth.

The IAA appropriated the stone, blocked the cave, and had plans to place it in the Israel Museum or Zippori National Park. We argued, with our lawyers, that the tomb was the property of Yehoshua Ben Levi, it has remained undisturbed for almost eighteen hundred years, and no one was granted the right to remove anything or make any changes. After a decade-long battle, the authorities accepted our view that it was better to leave the site as we found it. The tomb door

was returned and the cave restored. We signed papers and gave our pledge to allow access to all visitors who wish to come. It remains the only authenticated Mishnaic period rabbinical tomb in all of Galilee.

Today, many people come and go, including pilgrims seeking their own passageway to Paradise. Our family is proud to host the Ribal. We have always felt blessed in everything we have done here – our children, our farm, and the beautiful spot where we live have all thrived. We look after the Ribal, and we are assured that he looks after us as well. Wherever he is.

City of Mosaics

Zippori, the ancient Jewish capital of the Galilee, was not just a holy city of rabbis and the Sanhedrin (the rabbinical supreme court). It was also a beautiful, wealthy city built on a hillside in the Roman style, with many of its public buildings adorned with intricate mosaic floors.

Dozens of these floors remain and are on display today in Zippori National Park. They date from the second through the fifth centuries and feature wildly disparate subject matter ranging from the Temple in Jerusalem to Dionysius and beautiful women, together with scenes describing life along the Nile River in Egypt.

One large structure contains no less than a dozen different mosaic floors, almost per-

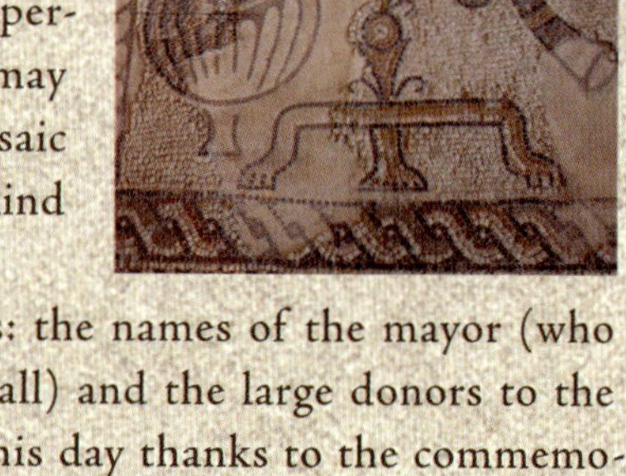

fectly preserved, which many believe may have been the headquarters of the mosaic makers' guild in Zippori, serving as a kind of showroom for customers.

Mosaics are also historical records: the names of the mayor (who reconstructed Zippori's pedestrian mall) and the large donors to the great synagogue are remembered to this day thanks to the commemorative mosaics they left behind.

The tradition continues to this day, with a mosaic tile workshop in Moshav Zippori passing on the techniques of this ancient craft.

Jewish Concept of the Afterlife

Rabbi Yehoshua Ben Levi probably wasn't surprised by what he found on arrival in Paradise: a supernal yeshiva attended by the souls of the great scholars, studying Torah for all eternity, with Elijah the Prophet serving as the heavenly concierge.

But it's all a matter of timing. Had the rabbi arrived in the Jewish Celestial City a thousand years earlier, he might have found nothing at all. Every age spawns its own concept of the afterlife. The generations of Jews who recorded their legacy in scrolls that we now call the Hebrew Bible didn't seem to attach much significance to a hereafter. And the forefathers never related to the concept of the afterworld during their lives.

The prophet Ezekiel raised this question to God as he surveyed the Valley of Dry Bones (Ezekiel 37:1). He was reassured about the eternity of Israel, although the prophecy relates to the people as a whole rather than any individual soul. The only spirit brought back from the other side was the Prophet Samuel, who seemed annoyed by the summons from King Saul (I Samuel 28:3) and neglected to mention from whence he came.

The celestial kingdom conceived by the rabbis of the Talmud has endured and remains the foundation of Jewish belief to this day. With his last breath, a pious Jew will recite the "Shema Yisrael" prayer with the expectation that he will be greeted on the other side by loved ones and ancestors. Together they all will await the coming of the Messiah, and all souls will be returned to a rebuilt Temple in Jerusalem. In the meantime, the scholars can pass the time studying Torah as a reward for a righteous life.

As part of this belief, many pious Jews will visit the tombs of the righteous, who are able to intervene in heavenly judgment. Candles are lit, Psalms recited, and notes left bearing specific requests and blessings.

On the door of the cave where Rabbi Yehoshua Ben Levi was interred at the start of his heavenly journey, there is a small slot that once served as a keyhole but today functions as a mailbox. The rabbi receives more mail every few days than he ever did in his lifetime.

While the majority of modern Jews are skeptical as to the abilities of deceased rabbis to intervene in our lives from the afterworld, there remains the possibility that it can't hurt either, so the phenomenon has grown and is widespread among certain Jewish communities today.

Henry Wadsworth Longfellow and the Jews

Every American schoolchild of a certain era memorized "one if by land, two if by sea." The great nineteenth-century American poet Henry Wadsworth Longfellow was very much part of the popular culture of his time.

More obscure was his interest in Judaism. He was especially intrigued by the traditions of the Spanish Jew, whom he saw as a bridge between the cultures of the Orient and the Western literary canon. Longfellow studied the ancient mystical Jewish wisdom of the Kabbalah and tried to master the Hebrew language as well. This resulted in his depiction of the Spanish Jew that appears in his collection *Tales of a Wayside Inn* and his poem "The Jewish Cemetery at Newport."

No doubt, Longfellow also had help from Jewish scholars, but his portrait of Rabbi Yoshua Ben Levi shows great sensitivity to the nuances of the Aramaic text and is very true to the legend as it appears in the Talmud.

About the Artist

Avi Katz was born in Philadelphia in 1949. After studying at the University of California, Berkeley, he moved to Israel in 1970, where he earned a Bachelor of Fine Arts at Bezalel Academy of Arts and Design. He started in painting and art teaching before turning to illustration full time. His drawings, ranging in style from realism to caricature and comics, graced the pages of the *Jerusalem Report* for three decades. He has illustrated hundreds of books; the *JPS Illustrated Children's Bible* won the National Jewish Book Award, and his books have received the Hans Christian Andersen Award four times. In 2020, Avi designed the mosaic mural telling the legend of Rabbi Yehoshua Ben Levi, overlooking his tomb in Zippori.

פינה מקום לבר לוי